MW00365912

Families Are Forever

A Year of Family Night Lessons and Activities to Strengthen Your Home

KIMIKO CHRISTENSEN HAMMARI

CFI
An imprint of Cedar Fort, Inc.
Springville, Utah

For Lilli June,
who makes our family complete.

ISBN 13: 978-1-4621-1300-2

Published by CFI, an imprint of Cedar Fort, Inc., 2373 W. 700 S., Springville, UT, 84663
Distributed by Cedar Fort, Inc., www.cedarfort.com

Cover design by Shawnda T. Craig
Cover design © 2013 by Lyle Mortimer
Edited by Shelby Law

Printed in the United States of America

10 9 8 7 6 5 4 3 2 1

Printed on acid-free paper

Contents

July

August

September

October

November

December

Fun Food for FHE

How to Use This Book

This book provides a year's worth of family home evening lessons that teach your children how to increase their faith in Jesus Christ and make good choices. In order to get the most out of this manual and reinforce what your children are learning in Primary, teach the lessons in order. The lessons are divided into monthly themes and subdivided into weekly themes. Four lessons are provided for each month, and each lesson is divided into the following sections:

Resources

Scriptures, Primary songs, hymns, and pictures from the Gospel Art Book. (Note: The Gospel Art Book is available at www.lds.org. You can download and print pictures or show the pictures to your children on the computer, if it is available during your lesson. You can order a copy of the Gospel Art Book at store.lds.org.

Lesson

A brief explanation of the theme is given with corresponding scriptures and discussion questions.

Activity

The activities are meant to reinforce what is taught in the lesson, so they may not be the games your family is used to playing. Most lessons include separate activities for younger children and older children. Generally, the activities for younger children are for ages three to seven, and the older children, eight to eleven. However, don't use this guideline as a firm rule. Some younger children may be advanced for their age, and some older children may still enjoy the activities for younger children. You know your children best, so present the activities that you think they will enjoy.

Challenge

These challenges should be completed during the week before the next Monday. At the beginning of each family home evening, follow up with your children on the previous week's challenge. Discuss their success and help them with any problems or concerns. Each lesson includes a challenge card that should be printed from the CD. Your children should fill out a card and put it somewhere they will see it during the week so they can be reminded of what to work on. The challenge cards include a line where your children can sign their names and formally commit to the challenge. This method will help your children understand that writing down a goal makes it a more solid commitment.

CD-ROM

The CD has been provided for your convenience in printing handouts, challenge cards, and other lesson materials. This entire book is available on the CD and can be printed in color. It is recommended that you print out activities and challenge cards from the CD so you don't have to write in your book or cut it up. A "Read Me" file on the CD explains how to use it.

January

Heavenly Father Prepared a Way
for Me to Return to His Presence

I am a child of God and can be like Him someday.

Lesson

Before we came to earth, we lived as spirits with Heavenly Father. He knew and loved us very much, just as He does now. He is the father of our spirits. That means we are literally children of God. Although we have parents here on earth, Heavenly Father will always be the father of our spirits. We cannot see Him, but He will always look out for us, just as our earthly parents do. He wants us to be happy and return to Him someday. He wants to bless us and give us all the wonderful things He has.

Read and discuss Romans 8:16–17.

+ What is an heir? What does it mean to be joint-heirs with Christ?
+ Why does Heavenly Father want to share His glory with us?

Resources

(Select one from each category.)

Children's Songbook
+ I Am a Child of God (2)
+ My Heavenly Father Loves Me (228)

Hymn
+ O My Father (292)
+ I Know My Father Lives (302)

Scriptures
+ Psalm 82:6
+ Galatians 4:7

Activity

Younger Children: Do the puzzle on page 4. Print it from the resource CD and cut out the pieces. Then put the puzzle back together.
Older Children: See page 5.

Challenge

Heavenly Father loves you and wants to hear from you often. Even though you can't see Him, you can pray to Him. Make a goal this week to make your daily prayers more sincere so your relationship with Him will grow. Express gratitude for your blessings, tell Him about the good things that happen to you, tell Him about your problems, and ask Him for help.

> ## Challenge
>
> This week, I commit to make my prayers to Heavenly Father more sincere. I will express my gratitude, tell Him about my day, and ask for help when I need it.
>
> _____
> Signature
>
> _____
> Date

4

Pick a Word

In each box, cross out all the words that are repeated until only one word remains. Place the remaining word on the blank line at the bottom of the page. After you have done this for each box, you will find the name of a popular Primary song. *Solution on page 142.*

6

GOT	GET	GONE
GONE	GOB	GOT
GET	GOD	GOB

3

A	I	AT
ID	IT	ID
I	AT	IT

2

AT	AH	AN
AD	AN	AD
AH	AT	AM

5

OF	ON	OR
OR	UN	DO
ON	DO	UN

1

AT	IN	IF
IF	I	A
IN	A	AT

4

CHAT	CHIVE	CHIT
CHIT	CHIDE	CHILD
CHIVE	CHAT	CHIDE

1. _____

2. _____

3. _____

4. _____

5. _____

6. _____

5

Heavenly Father provided a Savior so I can return to His presence.

Resources

(Select one from each category.)

Children's Songbook
- He Sent His Son (34)
- Beautiful Savior (62)

Hymn
- Redeemer of Israel (6)
- The Lord Is My Shepherd (108)

Gospel Art Book
- The Resurrected Jesus Christ (239)
- Jesus the Christ (240)

Scriptures
- 1 John 4:14
- D&C 43:34

Lesson

When Heavenly Father presented His plan to us, we were excited and shouted with joy. But we knew, and Heavenly Father knew, we could not complete our life on earth alone. No matter how hard we tried to keep the commandments, we would still make mistakes. We needed a Savior—someone who would save us from our sins.

Jesus Christ and Lucifer both offered to be our Savior. Lucifer wanted to force us to keep all the commandments, and he wanted to receive all the glory for it. Jesus, on the other hand, said He would let us grow by making our own choices. He would give His life for us in order to redeem us from our sins, and the glory would be His Father's. Heavenly Father chose Jesus to be our Savior and Redeemer.

Because Jesus gave His life for us, we have the freedom to choose right from wrong. When we make a mistake, we can repent and be forgiven. And if we have done that, someday we can return to live with Heavenly Father and Jesus forever. Jesus died for all the world, but He also died for you and me. He knows and loves us each individually. Because of this, you can say that Jesus is your personal Savior and Redeemer.

Read and discuss D&C 93:8–9.
- What is "the Word"?
- Why is Jesus called "the light and the Redeemer of the world"?

Activity

All Ages: Watch a video of the Savior. Many beautiful depictions of the Savior can be found at www.lds.org.

Challenge

Bear your testimony of Jesus Christ. It doesn't have to be during a formal occasion such as fast and testimony meeting. You can write it in your journal, share it with your family, or even bear it through your actions (being a good example).

Challenge

This week, I commit to bear my testimony of Jesus Christ to a family member or friend or through my actions.

_____
Signature

_____
Date

Jesus Christ is the perfect example for me to follow.

Resources

(Select one from each category.)

Children's Songbook
+ I'm Trying to Be Like Jesus (78)
+ Love One Another (136)

Hymn
+ The Lord Is My Light (89)
+ More Holiness Give Me (131)

Gospel Art Book
+ Christ's Image (1)
+ Christ with Children (116)

Scriptures
+ Matthew 4:19
+ John 13:15

Lesson

Jesus Christ is the perfect example of how to live because He lived a perfect life. He always obeyed Heavenly Father. He was kind and showed love to everyone, always putting others' needs before His own. When He visited the Nephites and told them it was time for Him to leave, He noticed how much they still needed Him and decided to stay longer. He told them, "Behold, my bowels are filled with compassion towards you" (3 Nephi 17:6). Then He invited anyone who was sick or afflicted to come to Him for a blessing. It did not matter to Him that He had planned on leaving. He loved these people and wanted to heal them.

If we follow Jesus's example, we will love and serve one another. We will have a greater desire to keep the commandments, and we will grow closer to Heavenly Father and Jesus Christ.

Read and discuss 3 Nephi 27:27.
+ To whom is Jesus speaking? Does this commandment apply to us as well?

8

- Why did Jesus give this commandment?
- What are you already doing to become like Jesus? What can you do better?

Activity

Younger Children: See page 10.
Older Children: See page 11.

Challenge

Jesus Christ is the perfect example for us, and we need to be a good example to others. Each day this week, find an opportunity to be a good example. This can include not fighting with your siblings, listening to your teacher at school, being kind to others, and so on.

Challenge

I will find an opportunity each day this week to be a good example.

_____
Signature

_____
Date

Hidden Message

Color each square with a ♡ in it. Then read the letters in the remaining squares, in order, to find a message that Jesus taught.

♡	♡	♡	♡	♡	♡	♡	♡	♡	♡
♡	♡	♡	L	♡	♡	♡	♡	O	♡
♡	V	♡	♡	♡	♡	♡	♡	♡	♡
♡	♡	♡	♡	E	♡	♡	♡	♡	♡
E	♡	♡	♡	♡	♡	♡	V	♡	♡
♡	♡	E	♡	♡	♡	R	♡	♡	♡
♡	♡	♡	Y	♡	♡	♡	♡	♡	♡
♡	♡	♡	♡	O	♡	♡	♡	♡	N
♡	♡	♡	♡	E	♡	♡	♡	♡	♡

I Can Be like Jesus

Below is a list of things that we can do to follow Jesus Christ's example. Find the words in bold in the word search. *Solution on page 142.*

BE **KIND** TO OTHERS
GO TO **CHURCH**
READ THE
   SCRIPTURES
PRAY OFTEN
DO **MISSIONARY**
   WORK
BE **OBEDIENT**
PAY **TITHING**
HELP THE **POOR**
VOLUNTEER OUR
   TIME
RESPECT OTHERS
BE **BAPTIZED**
GO TO THE **TEMPLE**
BE **REVERENT**
OBEY THE **WORD**
   OF WISDOM

```
B W F M Q Z G D B N J O H V E
S T O W O R D O F W I S D O M
C I M J H P M J K D I N V L S
R M X H U O T H I M P Q O R G
I E J G V O B B N Y W E B N R
P Z E H O R Z A D V L F I T E
T X P V P T W K P O S H Y W S
U T Q E R C O Q V T T M C N P
R E V R A P Y X O I I C H F E
E U N Z Y R G F T S A Z S D C
S M I S S I O N A R Y V E N T
M Q O L X Q M B B N C J O D P
E A O T U O B E D I E N T J L
C H U R C H W T E M P L E W Q
H C R E V E R E N T U A L Y I
```

I can return to Heavenly Father by following Jesus.

Lesson

Jesus said, "I am the way, the truth, and the life: no man cometh unto the Father, but by me" (John 14:6). Without Jesus Christ, we cannot return to Heavenly Father. Jesus set the perfect example for us, and we need to follow Him and keep the commandments. We need to love others as He did and serve people without expecting anything in return.

However, we will all fall short. We will all make mistakes and break the commandments. Because Jesus loves us, He died for us so that we can repent and be forgiven of our sins.

If we do our best to follow Jesus Christ, and repent when we do wrong, He will lead us back to Heavenly Father.

Read and discuss 2 Nephi 31:10.

+ How do we follow Jesus Christ?
+ Can we still follow Him if we disobey the commandments?

Resources

(Select one from each category.)

Children's Songbook
+ I Feel My Savior's Love (74)
+ I'm Trying to Be Like Jesus (78)

Hymn
+ The Lord Is My Light (89)
+ Come, Follow Me (116)

Gospel Art Book
+ The Sermon on the Mount (39)
+ Lord, Save Me (43)

Scriptures
+ Psalm 25:4
+ Matthew 8:18–22

Activity

All Ages: Cut out several sets of footprints (see page 14 for a pattern), and lead them from one room to another. Place something appealing at the end of the footprints, such as a good book or a treat. Instruct your children to walk on the footprints and follow them to a prize. At the end, discuss how following Jesus Christ leads us back to Heavenly Father.

Challenge

With your family, talk about attributes of the Savior that you would like to master. Pick one and strive to develop it this week. Realize that you won't be perfect, but strive each day to do your best.

Challenge

This week my family and I will strive to develop the following attribute: _____.

_____

Signature

_____

Date

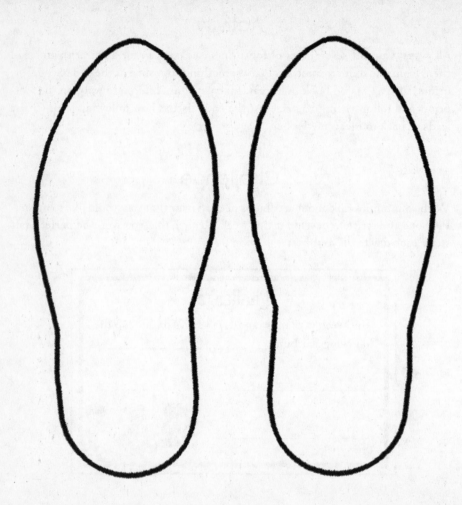

February

Heavenly Father Has a Plan
for His Children

Resources

(Select one from each category.)

Children's Songbook
- I Am a Child of God (2)
- I Lived in Heaven (4)

Hymn
- O My Father (292)
- I Am a Child of God (301)

Gospel Art Book
- The Earth (3)

Scriptures
- Alma 42:13
- Moses 6:62

Heavenly Father has a plan for His children.

Lesson

Heavenly Father loves us very much. He wants us to feel joy and to have everything that He has. But when we lived with Him as spirits in the pre-mortal world, we did not have bodies like He has. And because we had always lived with Him, we hadn't experienced certain things that would help us to grow.

Heavenly Father created a plan for each of us. It is called the plan of salvation. Through this plan, we all chose to come to earth and gain a physical body. We chose to follow Jesus Christ and keep the commandments. If we do this, we will return to live with Heavenly Father after we die. We will have great joy because we will have become like Him.

Read and discuss Moses 1:39.
- What is God's "work and glory"?
- What does it mean to "bring to pass the immortality and eternal life of man"?

16

Activity

All Ages: Play a game of kickball or baseball. Have each base represent a step in the plan of salvation (first base: earth life, second base: death, third base: the spirit world, home plate: final judgment/celestial kingdom). Explain to your children that just like in life, there will be obstacles and challenges in this game. The opposing team will try to get you out, and you must do all you can to make it to safety.

Challenge

With your family, memorize the song, "I Will Follow God's Plan" (*Children's Songbook*, 164).

Challenge

This week I will memorize, "I Will Follow God's Plan."

_____

Signature

_____

Date

Heavenly Father commanded Jesus Christ to create the earth.

Resources

(Select one from each category.)

Children's Songbook
+ My Heavenly Father Loves Me (228)
+ All Things Bright and Beautiful (231)

Hymn
+ All Creatures of Our God and King (62)
+ For the Beauty of the Earth (92)

Gospel Art Book
+ The Lord Created All Things (2)
+ The Earth (3)

Scriptures
+ John 1:10
+ Colossians 1:16

Lesson

As part of the plan of happiness, we needed a place where we could receive a physical body and be tested. Jesus Christ created the earth under the direction of Heavenly Father. We are here on earth to learn and grow and take care of our physical bodies.

Jesus Christ created many wonderful things for us to enjoy here on earth. Let's read about the creation of the earth in Genesis chapter 1.

Read and discuss Genesis 1.
+ What did Jesus create first? Last?
+ Why did He rest on the seventh day?

Activity

Younger Children: Draw a picture of your favorite animal that Jesus created.

Older Children: Draw a picture of what happened each day of the Creation.

Challenge

Each day this week, write in your journal (or draw a picture) about one of Jesus Christ's creations that you are thankful for.

Challenge

Each day this week, I will write in my journal (or draw a picture) about a creation that I am thankful for.

_____

Signature

_____

Date

My body is created in the image of God.

Lesson

Resources

(Select one from each category.)

Children's Songbook
+ I Am a Child of God (2)
+ The Lord Gave Me a Temple (153)

Hymn
+ Sweet Is the Peace the Gospel Brings (14)
+ Keep the Commandments (303)

Gospel Art Book
+ Young Boy Praying (111)
+ Christ and Children from around the World (116)

Scriptures
+ Mosiah 2:37
+ Ether 3:16

Before we came to earth, we lived in heaven with our Heavenly Father. We were His spirit children. Heavenly Father wanted us to have physical bodies like His so that we could become more like Him. He and Jesus Christ created the earth so that we would have a place to receive a body.

In the Old Testament, we learn that "God created man in his own image, in the image of God created he him; male and female created he them" (Genesis 1:27). Heavenly Father created us to look like Him. He has a body of flesh and bone, just as we do. He has a head and arms and legs and a face just like we do. The Prophet Joseph Smith testified of this when Heavenly Father and Jesus Christ appeared to him in the Sacred Grove. Joseph Smith said that he saw two personages and that they were men similar to us.

Our bodies are a sacred gift from Heavenly Father. We need to show respect to them and take good care of them.

Read and discuss D&C 130:22.

- What is God's body made of?
- How is your body like Heavenly Father's?

Activity

All Ages: Our bodies are a gift from Heavenly Father, and we need to take care of them. Eating nutritious foods is one of the most important things we can do for our bodies. Prepare a healthy snack together as a family.

Challenge

One of the ways we can take care of our bodies is to keep them active. This week, do three things to keep your body active: go for a walk, play a game of soccer, ride your bike, and so on.

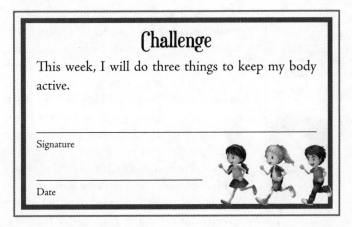

Challenge

This week, I will do three things to keep my body active.

_____

Signature

_____

Date

Agency is the gift to choose for myself.

Lesson

In the scriptures, we read that men are "agents unto themselves" (Moses 6:56). That means each of us has the ability to make choices for ourselves. No one can force us to do anything against our will.

Before we came to earth, there was a great war in heaven. When Heavenly Father presented the plan of happiness, He told us that we would need to make good choices in order to return to Him. But Heavenly Father knew it would not be easy and that we would need a savior. Lucifer said that he would be our savior and force us to keep the commandments so we could return to Heavenly Father. But that was not a good plan because we wouldn't have the freedom to choose. Jesus Christ said He would be our savior and teach us the right way. Then we would each decide which path to take. Heavenly Father was very pleased with this plan, and so were we. We chose to come to earth and follow Jesus Christ.

Here on earth, we are faced with choices each day. We have the freedom to choose between right and wrong, and we will be responsible for our choices. If

Resources

(Select one from each category.)

Children's Songbook
+ Nephi's Courage (120)
+ Dare to Do Right (158)

Hymn
+ Choose the Right (239)
+ Teach Me to Walk in the Light (304)

Gospel Art Book
+ Adam and Eve Teaching Their Children (5)
+ Family Prayer (112)

Scriptures
+ D&C 101:78
+ Articles of Faith 1:2

we choose the right, we will be blessed. If we choose to sin, we will have to suffer the consequences.

Read and discuss Helaman 14:29–31.
+ What happens if we make good choices?
+ What happens if we choose evil?

Activity

All Ages: Fill a large suitcase or a garbage bag with various items of clothing. Ask your children to close their eyes and choose three items of clothing from the bag. No matter what they choose, tell them that that is the outfit they have to wear the next day. Ask them how they feel about not getting a choice. Discuss the importance of agency and reiterate that it is a great gift from Heavenly Father.

Challenge

Each time you make a decision this week, stop and ask yourself if it is a good choice or a bad choice. Ask yourself if your decision will help you grow closer to the Savior. (Keep in mind that some decisions are neither good nor bad. Heavenly Father isn't concerned about whether you wear a blue shirt or a red shirt. However, he is concerned about how you choose to treat people or what kind of movies you watch.) See page 24 for the challenge card.

Challenge

This week, before I make a decision, I will stop and ask myself it is a good choice or a bad choice.

_____
Signature

_____
Date

March

Jesus Christ Is
Our Savior

I can gain a testimony of Jesus Christ.

Lesson

Heavenly Father wants us all to have our own testimony of Jesus Christ. That means He wants us all to know for ourselves that Jesus Christ is our Savior. Someone can tell us that Jesus Christ is our Savior, but we have to believe it and know it for ourselves. We each have to have our own witness from the Holy Ghost that Jesus Christ lives.

Gaining a testimony is a process. It doesn't happen overnight. We have to go to church, read the scriptures, and pray before we can gain a testimony. When we do these things, we will feel peace from the Holy Ghost, and our testimony will grow.

Read and discuss Alma 7:13.

+ What was Alma's testimony?
+ How can you develop a testimony of the Savior?

Activity

All Ages: Write down your testimony of the Savior and send it to a friend or relative in a letter. Explain

Resources

(Select one from each category.)

Children's Songbook
+ Jesus Has Risen (70)
+ Search, Ponder, and Pray (109)

Hymn
+ I Know that My Redeemer Lives (136)
+ Testimony (137)

Gospel Art Book
+ Living Water (36)
+ Go Ye Therefore, and Teach All Nations (61)

Scriptures
+ Psalm 19:7
+ D&C 76:22

26

why Jesus Christ is important to you. If you don't know how to write yet, you can draw a picture and have a parent write a message on it.

Challenge

The prophets have borne powerful testimonies about the Savior. Read and discuss "The Living Christ" as a family (available on www.lds.org).

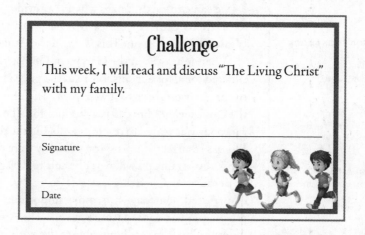

Challenge

This week, I will read and discuss "The Living Christ" with my family.

_____
Signature

_____
Date

Through the Atonement I can repent and be forgiven of my sins.

Resources

(Select one from each category.)

Children's Songbook
+ He Sent His Son (34)
+ He Died That We Might Live Again (65)

Hymn
+ I Know That My Redeemer Lives (136)
+ Jesus, Once of Humble Birth (196)

Gospel Art Book
+ Christ in Gethsemane (56)
+ The Crucifixion (57)

Scriptures
+ John 3:16
+ Helaman 5:9

Lesson

Heavenly Father knew we would make mistakes when we came to earth. That's why He provided a Savior for us. Jesus Christ died for us so that we can live with Heavenly Father again. This is called the Atonement.

When Jesus was in the Garden of Gethsemane, He suffered for all of our sins. He paid the price of our sins so that we won't have to if we repent. Then He died on the cross, giving Himself as a sacrifice for all mankind. His body was placed to rest in a tomb. On the third day, He was resurrected. His spirit and body were reunited. He is alive again and will never be able to die again.

Because of Christ's great gift to us, we will be resurrected someday. But more important, we can repent and be cleansed from our sins. The Atonement of Jesus Christ makes it possible to live with Heavenly Father again.

Read and discuss Helaman 5:9.
+ How did Jesus Christ redeem the world?
+ Why is He the only way back to our Heavenly Father?

28

Activity

Younger Children: Fill a jar with water and tell your children that the water represents their spirit. Then add a couple drops of food coloring, which represents sin. Stir the water until the food coloring dyes all of the water. Explain that when we sin, our spirits get "dirty." Add some bleach to the jar and watch the color disappear. Explain that through the Atonement, we can be washed clean from our sins.
Older Children: See page 34.

Challenge

During family scripture study this week, read the parable of the prodigal son in Luke 15:11–32. Discuss the following with your family: What was the turning point for the prodigal son? How did his father react when he returned home? How did his brother react? Which man reacted the way Jesus would?

Challenge

This week, I will read and discuss Luke 15:11–32 with my family.

_____

Signature

_____

Date

Resources

(Select one from each category.)

Children's Songbook
+ Did Jesus Really Live Again? (64)
+ The Lord Gave Me a Temple (153)

Hymn
+ My Redeemer Lives (135)
+ He Is Risen (199)

Gospel Art Book
+ Why Weepest Thou? (59)
+ Behold My Hands and Feet (60)

Scriptures
+ Matthew 28:6
+ Alma 40:23

Jesus Christ was resurrected, and I will be too.

Lesson

When Jesus Christ died on the cross for us, His body was placed in a tomb. On the third day, when His disciples went to check on Him, they found His tomb empty. Jesus had overcome death and had been resurrected. His spirit and His body were reunited.

Through the Atonement of Jesus Christ, we too will be resurrected. Our spirits and our bodies will come together again and will be perfected. We will no longer suffer illness or injury. For example, a blind man will be able to see again. A deaf man will hear again. Someone who lost a leg in this life will be able to walk and run perfectly. Resurrection is a gift to everyone on this earth because Heavenly Father and Jesus love us so much.

Read and discuss Mosiah 16:6–9.

+ How is death "swallowed up in Christ"?
+ Why does "the grave hath no victory"?
+ In verse 9, we read that "there can be no more death." Does this mean that since Christ was resurrected no one can die anymore?

30

Activity

All Ages, Option 1: Visit the grave of a family member or friend and take flowers to decorate it. While you are there, discuss what you learned in this lesson.

All Ages, Option 2: Look at pictures of your ancestors or others who have passed away. Who are you excited to see again? Talk about what you will say to them when you see them again.

Challenge

The resurrection is a very important part of the gospel. This week, find a scripture about the resurrection not discussed in this lesson. Share it with your family next week during family home evening. An older sibling or parent may help you.

Challenge

I will share the following scripture about the resurrection with my family next week:

_____

_____

Signature

_____

Date

I can show respect for the Savior by being reverent.

Lesson

Resources

(Select one from each category.)

Children's Songbook
+ Reverently, Quietly (26)
+ I Want to Be Reverent (28)

Hymn
+ Oh, May My Soul Commune with Thee (123)
+ Reverently and Meekly Now (185)

Gospel Art Book
+ Passing the Sacrament (108)
+ Young Boy Praying (111)

Scriptures
+ Psalm 89:7
+ D&C 107:4

Imagine your family is having fun playing a board game at the kitchen table. Your friend walks in the front door, comes over to the table, and throws the game and the pieces on the floor. Then he starts yelling at everyone and ruins your perfect evening. How would you feel? What would you do? Most likely, you would be very upset and ask him why he did that. You might explain to him that your family was enjoying time together and that he disrupted it. You might also explain to your friend that your feelings are hurt because he did not respect you and your family.

Jesus Christ feels the same way when we are not reverent at church. Being reverent means sitting quietly and listening. It means keeping our hands still and not making noise. By being reverent, we show our love and respect for Jesus. When we are not reverent, our actions tell Him that we don't love Him enough to quietly listen to the lesson. We show Him that talking to a friend or misbehaving is more important than His gospel.

What can you do this week to show reverence?

Read and discuss Hebrews 12:28.

+ What is reverence? What is godly fear?
+ How can we show reverence and godly fear for God?

Activity

All Ages: Play Dead Fish. First, give your children a chance to get out their wiggles and giggles. Then have each of them lie on the ground, as still and as quietly as they can be. Mom or Dad watches each child closely. Anyone who moves or makes noises is out. The last remaining "dead fish" wins. When the game is over, discuss the following as a family: How is pretending to be a dead fish like being reverent? How can we be reverent? Explain that being reverent does not mean we have to pretend to be a dead fish at church. Discuss the times it is appropriate to speak or move around at church.

Challenge

Next Sunday, make a special effort to be reverent during Primary and sacrament meeting. When you are tempted to talk or move around, think about Jesus.

Challenge

I promise to be reverent during Primary and sacrament meeting next Sunday.

_____
Signature

_____
Date

Crossword Puzzle

THE ATONEMENT

Solution on page 142.

DOWN

2. Jesus's sacrifice is called the _____.
3. God forgives us for our sins when we _____.
4. After Jesus died, His body was _____.
5. Jesus died on the _____.
7. Jesus will never be able to _____ again.

ACROSS

1. Jesus offered Himself as a _____ for us.
6. When we break the commandments, we _____.
8. Another name for Jesus Christ
9. The Atonement is the greatest _____ God has given us.
10. Jesus prayed in the _____ of Gethsemane.

34

April

The Family Is Central to God's Plan

The family is central to God's plan.

Lesson

Resources

(Select one from each category.)

Children's Songbook
+ The Hearts of the Children (92)
+ I Love to See the Temple (95)

Hymn
+ Home Can Be a Heaven on Earth (298)
+ Families Can Be Together Forever (300)

Gospel Art Book
+ Adam and Eve Teaching Their Children (5)
+ Family Prayer (112)

Scriptures
+ Malachi 4:6
+ D&C 138:48

What would your life be like without your family? It would get pretty lonely, wouldn't it? And it would be pretty scary at times. We need families for many reasons. Families take care of each other and give each other support. But the most important reason for having a family is that families are central to Heavenly Father's plan.

From the beginning of time, families have lived on the earth. Adam and Eve were the first family. They were commanded to have children and found much joy as their family grew.

Another righteous family in the scriptures is Lehi and Sariah's family in the Book of Mormon. God commanded Lehi to take his family into the wilderness and start a new life. Jerusalem, the city where they lived, was full of wicked people and was about to be destroyed. God wanted to save this family because they were righteous. Even though Laman and Lemuel complained a lot, they went with their family. The family had many trials during their journey, but they worked together to fulfill God's plan.

Read and discuss 1 Nephi 2:4.

♦ What did Lehi and his family have to leave behind? What did they take with them?

♦ Imagine your family had to do something similar and that you didn't have anything left except each other. Name one strength that each member of your family has that would help your family survive.

Activity

Younger Children: On page 38, you'll find a picture of an empty house. Draw pictures or write phrases that represent a happy family.
Older Children: See page 39.

Challenge

Show someone in your family how much you love him or her. You could help your parents with extra chores, share your toys with your siblings, write a nice letter, or simply tell your family members that you love them.

Challenge

This week, I will show one of my family members how much I love him or her.

_____
Signature

_____
Date

A Happy Family

Unscramble the words in the list below to spell words that relate to a happy family. *Solution on page 142.*

1. TNIUY

2. VOLE

3. RBRHTEO

4. TOHMRE

5. SRITSE

6. OEMH

7. TAHFER

8. YAMILF

1. _____

2. _____

3. _____

4. _____

5. _____

6. _____

7. _____

8. _____

Week TWO

Parents have important responsibilities in families.

Resources

(Select one from each category.)

Children's Songbook
+ My Mother Dear (203)
+ Fathers (209)

Hymn
+ O My Father (292)
+ Teach Me to Walk in the Light (304)

Gospel Art Book
+ Adam and Eve Teaching Their Children (5)

Scriptures
+ Moroni 8:10
+ Moses 6:54

Lesson

Why do you think Heavenly Father gave you parents? Was it so that you had someone to boss you around and make you do your chores? Or did He provide us each with parents so we have loving adults to protect us and help us learn and grow?

The prophets have taught that being a parent is a very sacred responsibility. Parents are raising Heavenly Father's spirit children. They need to provide food, shelter, clothing, and other necessities for their children. But more important, they need to provide a loving home where the Holy Ghost can dwell, and where the children can learn about Jesus Christ. Parents need to set a good example and teach their children how to pray and study the scriptures. When we see how much our parents love us, we can better understand how much Heavenly Father loves us.

Read and discuss Mosiah 4:14–15.
+ What are parents' responsibilities?
+ How can you help your parents fulfill their responsibilities?

Activity

Younger Children: Go on a picture scavenger hunt. Look for pictures in magazines or books that show parents and their children. The first person to find five pictures wins.

Older Children: Go on a scripture scavenger hunt. Look for scriptures that talk about parents' responsibilities. The first person to find five scriptures wins.

Challenge

Show your parents how much you appreciate them. Draw them a picture, write them a note, or do an act of service for them.

Challenge

This week, I will show my parents how much I appreciate them.

_____
Signature

_____
Date

Children have the responsibility to obey their parents.

Lesson

Resources

(Select one from each category.)

Children's Songbook
+ Love Is Spoken Here (190)
+ The Family (194)

Hymn
+ Home Can Be a Heaven on Earth (298)
+ Teach Me to Walk in the Light (304)

Gospel Art Book
+ Family Prayer (112)

Scriptures
+ Proverbs 4:1
+ Colossians 3:20

All members of a family have great responsibilities. Last week, we talked about parents' responsibilities. What do you think your responsibilities are as a child?

One of the Ten Commandments states, "Honour thy father and thy mother" (Exodus 20:12). That means you should show your parents respect and obey them. All parents have rules, and sometimes they have to give consequences when we don't follow them. But they only do that because they love us. They want us to be obedient and keep the commandments so our family can be together forever.

When children obey their parents, there is love and harmony in the home. It is easier to feel the Spirit and follow Jesus Christ.

Read and discuss Ephesians 6:1.
+ What does it mean to "obey your parents in the Lord"?
+ How do you think your parents feel when you disobey them?

42

Activity

All Ages: This week, let your parents choose an activity that they'd like to do as a family. It may not be something you enjoy, but respect your parents' wishes and try to have a good time.

Challenge

This week, practice the commandment "Honor thy father and thy mother." You might be tempted to argue when they ask you to do your chores or go to bed, but make a special effort to be humble and obey your parents.

Challenge

This week, I will obey my parents every time they ask me to do something.

_____
Signature

_____
Date

I can show love to each member of my family.

Lesson

Our families are one of the greatest gifts our Heavenly Father has given us. Without them we would be lost and very lonely. As with all precious gifts, we need to treasure it and strengthen our family relationships.

We can show our love for our family members in many different ways. In addition to saying, "I love you," or giving a hug, we can show our family that we love them by doing these simple things:

+ obeying our parents
+ serving each other
+ sharing with our siblings
+ including everyone when we're playing a game
+ reading to a younger sibling
+ writing notes or drawing pictures for each other

There are countless ways to show our love for each other. How do you show yours?

Read and discuss John 13:34–35.

Resources

(Select one from each category.)

Children's Songbook
+ Jesus Said Love Everyone (61)
+ Love One Another (136)

Hymn
+ Each Life That Touches Ours for Good (293)
+ Love at Home (294)

Scriptures
+ 1 John 4:20
+ Moroni 7:47

- What commandment did Jesus give His disciples?
- How can we show our love to each other?

Activity

All Ages: Put each family member's name in a paper bag. Take turns drawing a name. When each name is drawn, take turns saying something nice about that person.

Challenge

Find a way to serve a family member this week. You could do chores for a sibling, spend time with a family member who is sad, write a note to one of the family members, and so on.

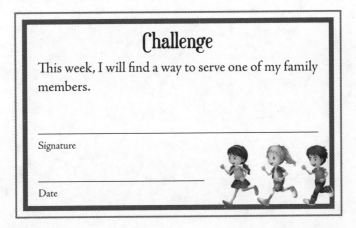

Challenge

This week, I will find a way to serve one of my family members.

_____
Signature

_____
Date

May

Families Are Blessed When They Follow the Prophet

God speaks to us through prophets.

Lesson

The prophet is often called the Lord's mouth-piece because he tells us the mind and the will of the Lord. He tells us what God would tell us if He were here.

Moses told Pharaoh to free the children of Israel. Lehi commanded the people of Jerusalem to repent. Today, we are led by living prophets. Thomas S. Monson is the president of the Church. He has two counselors and twelve apostles. All of these men are considered prophets. They have told us to repent of our sins, hold family home evening, and obtain food storage. Whenever the prophet speaks, we should treat his words as God's own words.

Read and discuss D&C 1:38.

+ Why does God speak through prophets?
+ How should we treat the prophets' words?

Resources

(Select one from each category.)

Children's Songbook
+ The Seventh Article of Faith (126b)
+ Seek the Lord Early (108)

Hymn
+ The Voice of God Again Is Heard (18)
+ Hark, All Ye Nations! (264)

Scriptures
+ 1 Nephi 22:1–2
+ D&C 43:1–7

Activity

All Ages, Option 1: Play Latter-day Apostle Memory Match (see pages 50 and 51). Print the cards from the resource CD and cut them out. Place them face down on a table and take turns trying to match the picture of the apostle with the description of him.

All Ages, Option 2: Watch the biography of Thomas S. Monson, available at http://www.lds.org/media-library/video/feature-films.

Challenge

Learn the names of the members of the First Presidency and members of the Quorum of the Twelve Apostles.

Challenge

This week, I will learn the names of the members of the First Presidency and members of the Quorum of the Twelve Apostles.

_____
Signature

_____
Date

---

1 Boyd K. Packer	2 L. Tom Perry	3 Russell M. Nelson	4 Dallin H. Oaks
		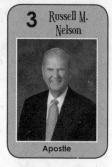	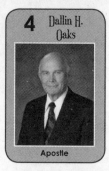
Apostle	Apostle	Apostle	Apostle
5 M. Russell Ballard	6 Richard G. Scott	7 Robert D. Hales	8 Jeffrey R. Holland
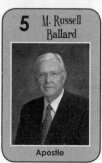			
Apostle	Apostle	Apostle	Apostle
9 David A. Bednar	10 Quentin L. Cook	11 D. Todd Christofferson	12 Neil L. Anderson
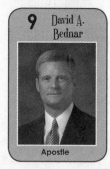			
Apostle	Apostle	Apostle	Apostle

Photos courtesy of newsroom.lds.org

1

Acting President of the Quorum of the Twelve—he formerly worked in education.

2

He was born in Logan, Utah, and spent his career in the retail business.

3

He was a heart surgeon and operated on President Spencer W. Kimball.

4

He was a lawyer, president of Brigham Young University, and justice of the Utah Supreme Court.

5

He served as a mission president in Canada. Much of his work as an apostle has been with missionary work.

6

In his talks, he often speaks of keeping our bodies and minds pure (law of chastity).

7

He earned a degree from Harvard and served in the U.S. Air Force as a jet fighter pilot.

8

He was a varsity athlete at Dixie High School and Dixie College.

9

He was serving as president of BYU—Idaho when he was called to be an apostle.

10

He has been the vice chairman of Sutter Health System and a business lawyer.

11

He served a mission to Argentina and later worked as a lawyer.

12

He is our newest apostle. He was sustained at the April 2009 general conference.

Resources

(Select one from each category.)

Children's Songbook
+ Seek the Lord Early (108)
+ Book of Mormon Stories (118)

Hymn
+ 'Twas Witnessed in the Morning Sky (12)
+ We Listen to a Prophet's Voice (22)

Gospel Art Book
+ Abraham Taking Isaac to Be Sacrificed (9)

Scriptures
+ 1 Nephi 4:2
+ Alma 48:17

The prophets in the scriptures are examples to my family.

Lesson

In the Old Testament, we read of a prophet named Abraham. He and his wife, Sariah, wanted a child very much, but Sariah was not able to have children. After many years, when Abraham and Sariah were both old, Sariah gave birth to a boy named Isaac. It was a miracle! Abraham and Sariah felt great joy and were very grateful to Heavenly Father.

When Isaac was older, God commanded Abraham to take Isaac up a mountain and sacrifice him. Abraham didn't want to. He loved Isaac very much. But he also trusted God and wanted to obey Him.

Abraham took Isaac up a mountain and built an altar. He laid his son on the altar and was ready to sacrifice him. An angel appeared to him and stopped him, saying that God was only testing Abraham.

Abraham is a great example of obedience. God asked him to do something very, very hard, and he was willing, even though it made him very sad. If we are obedient like Abraham was, we will be greatly blessed.

Read and discuss Genesis 22:15–18.

+ How was Abraham blessed for being obedient to the Lord?
+ What blessings will our family receive if we are obedient?

Activity

All Ages: Play a game of charades and act out different stories found in the scriptures. You can use the list below for ideas or come up with your own.

Noah   Moses   Nephi

King Benjamin   Alma   Moroni

Challenge

As a family, read about another prophet in the scriptures who is a good example.

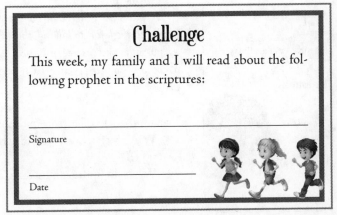

Challenge

This week, my family and I will read about the following prophet in the scriptures:

_____

Signature

_____

Date

My family will be blessed as we follow the prophet.

Lesson

When Nephi and his family were searching for the promised land, the Lord told them, "Inasmuch as ye shall keep my commandments ye shall prosper in the land; but inasmuch as ye will not keep my commandments ye shall be cut off from my presence" (2 Nephi 1:20). The same promise applies to each of us. When we follow the prophet and obey the commandments, Heavenly Father will bless us.

[Explain to your children some of the blessings you have received for following the prophet. Be as specific as possible and use terms they can understand. Then ask them how they have been blessed by following the prophet.]

Read and discuss Doctrine and Covenants 82:10.

+ Why is the Lord bound when we do what He says?
+ What does it mean to "have no promise"?

Resources

(Select one from each category.)

Children's Songbook
+ Follow the Prophet (110)
+ Nephi's Courage (120)

Hymn
+ We Ever Pray for Thee (23)
+ Praise to the Man (27)

Gospel Art Book
+ The Ten Commandments (14)
+ Moses and the Brass Serpent (16)

Scriptures
+ 2 Nephi 9:48
+ D&C 78:18

Activity

All Ages: Organize a commandments treasure hunt for your children, hiding each clue in a place that relates to counsel from the prophet. Older children should help the younger ones and help them figure out the clues. Place a treat or another reward at the end of the hunt. Explain to your children the correlation between the treasure hunt and how we are blessed for keeping the commandments.

You can use the following clues or come up with your own:

+ No other gods before me (hide the clue near a picture of the Savior)
+ Keep the Sabbath day holy (near a calendar or someone's church shoes)
+ Honor thy father and mother (in parents' room or on their bed)
+ Pay your tithing (near a piggy bank)
+ Keep the Word of Wisdom (on the refrigerator)
+ Dress modestly (in someone's closet or dresser)

Challenge

Memorize "Follow the Prophet" (*Children's Songbook*, 110).

Challenge

This week, I will memorize "Follow the Prophet."

_____

Signature

_____

Date

The prophet speaks to us at general conference.

Lesson

April and October are important months. On the first weekend of these months, we get to listen to the prophet and apostles speak to us in general conference. They pray beforehand to know what Heavenly Father wants them to say. Because of this, they are speaking for Heavenly Father.

General conference takes place in Salt Lake City at the Conference Center on Temple Square. Thousands of people go there to listen to the prophets and apostles. But there are many people in the world, and not everyone can go to Salt Lake City. Those of us who don't attend general conference in person can watch it on television or on the Internet. We can even listen to it on the radio. No matter where we live, we can listen to the prophet and apostles speak, and we can hear the word of God.

Read and discuss Amos 3:7.

+ What are some of the things the prophet and apostles have taught recently in general conference?
+ How can we hear conference talks if we can't go to Salt Lake City?

Resources

(Select one from each category.)

Children's Songbook
+ The Sixth Article of Faith (126a)
+ Latter-day Prophets (134)

Hymn
+ We Thank Thee, O God, for a Prophet (19)
+ God Bless Our Prophet Dear (24)

Gospel Art Book
+ Thomas S. Monson (137)

Scriptures
+ D&C 1:38
+ Articles of Faith 1:6

Activity

All ages: As a family, read or watch a conference talk. Make a poster with words or pictures that represent the talk. Hang it in the dining room or another prominent place where you will see it often and be reminded of the prophet's words.

Challenge

Each day, look at the poster that your family created for this week's activity. Think about what you can do to follow the prophet.

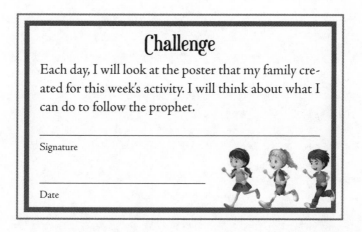

Challenge

Each day, I will look at the poster that my family created for this week's activity. I will think about what I can do to follow the prophet.

_____
Signature

_____
Date

June

Priesthood Ordinances and
Temple Work Bless My Family

Resources

(Select one from each category.)

Children's Songbook
+ The Priesthood Is Restored (89)
+ The Fifth Article of Faith (125)

Hymn
+ Praise to the Man (27)
+ Hark, All Ye Nations (264)

Gospel Art Book
+ Young Man Being Baptized (103)
+ Salt Lake Temple (119)

Scriptures
+ 3 Nephi 11:21
+ D&C 68:8

Priesthood ordinances bless and strengthen my family.

Lesson

Priesthood ordinances bless and strengthen our family. Ordinances include taking the sacrament, being baptized, receiving the gift of the Holy Ghost, and being endowed in the temple. All of these ordinances prepare us for the greatest ordinance of all: being sealed to our family for time and all eternity.

When we receive these priesthood ordinances, we make sacred covenants with Heavenly Father. We promise to serve Him and keep the commandments. We promise to stand as a witness of Jesus Christ.

When we are sealed in the temple, we promise to love each other and do all we can to help each other make it back to Heavenly Father.

When we honor our covenants, we have the constant companionship of the Holy Ghost. We have peace in our home, and our love for each other grows.

Read and discuss D&C 136:4.

+ What is our covenant?
+ What does it mean to "walk in all the ordinances of the Lord"?

Activity

All Ages: Watch one of the Bible videos on lds.org that shows Jesus using the priesthood. Videos are available at https://www.lds.org/media-library/video/bible-videos-the-life-of-jesus-christ?lang=eng.

Challenge

Show your appreciation to a priesthood holder. You could write him a note, make him a treat, draw him a picture, or do something that will make his calling easier that week.

Challenge

This week, I will show my appreciation to a priesthood holder.

_____
Signature

_____
Date

Temples make it possible for families to be together forever.

Lesson

Have you ever thought about what life would be like without your family? Maybe someone in your family has died, or maybe you know someone who has had a family member die. Losing someone you love is very difficult. Heavenly Father understands this, and He doesn't want families to be separated. We may lose our loved ones through death, but Heavenly Father has prepared a way for families to be together again after this life.

Families who are sealed in the temple will be together forever. Husbands and wives will be married forever, and their children will still belong to them after they die. But what about those who die before they get a chance to go to the temple? We can do their temple work for them and seal them to their families. Heavenly Father wants every family who has ever lived or will live on this earth to be an eternal family.

Read and discuss Helaman 10:7.

+ What does it mean to be sealed in the temple?
+ Why are temples important to the plan of salvation?

Resources

(Select one from each category.)

Children's Songbook
+ The Hearts of the Children (92)
+ I Love to See the Temple (95)

Hymn
+ How Beautiful Thy Temples, Lord (288)
+ Families Can Be Together Forever (300)

Gospel Art Book
+ Young Couple Going to the Temple (120)
+ Temple Baptismal Font (121)

Scriptures
+ D&C 2
+ D&C 128:15

Activity

All Ages: As a family, go to www.ldschurchtemples.com/construction. Find the temple currently under construction that is closest to your home. Show your children on a map where it is in relation to the city you live in. If you live close enough, make a goal to attend the open house or dedication when the temple is complete. (This may be two or three years away, but it will be a good lesson on how we need to wait and prepare to go to the temple.)

Challenge

The prophets have taught that our homes should be holy like a temple. Our homes should be a place where the Spirit can dwell. This week, help your family make your home holy like a temple. Be kind to each other, listen to good music, only watch wholesome things on TV, and so on.

Challenge

This week, I will help my family make our home holy like a temple.

_____
Signature

_____
Date

I can prepare now to be worthy to enter the temple.

Lesson

The temple is a very sacred place. It is the house of God. Because of that, we have to be worthy to enter it. That means we have to be clean spiritually and live the gospel. In addition, we need to be mature enough, or old enough, to understand the ordinances and sacred covenants that we make in the temple.

When Howard W. Hunter was the prophet, he wanted every member of the Church to have a temple recommend, even if they didn't live near a temple. He knew that living worthily would bless their lives, even if they couldn't attend the temple. When you are twelve years old, you can get a limited use recommend and do baptisms for the dead. In the meantime, you can prepare for that day. It is still important to live the gospel so that when you are old enough to go to the temple you don't have to change your habits.

How can we prepare to go to the temple?

Read and discuss Mormon 9:29.

- How do we "do all things in worthiness"?
- Why must we be worthy to enter the temple?

Resources

(Select one from each category.)

Children's Songbook
- I Want to Live the Gospel (148)
- I Have a Family Tree (199)

Hymn
- The Day Dawn Is Breaking (52)
- God Is in His Holy Temple (132)

Gospel Art Book
- Salt Lake Temple (119)
- Temple Baptismal Font (121)

Scriptures
- Psalm 24:3–4
- Moroni 10:32

64

Activity

All Ages: Give each child a straw, an empty bowl, and a bowl of M&Ms or Skittles. Give your children 30 seconds to suck up three pieces of orange candy with the straw and place them in the empty bowl. When they are finished, explain that just as there was a time limit in this game, we have a limited amount of time to prepare to go to the temple. We have been given specific instructions on how to prepare. In this game, the instructions were to place only the orange candy in the bowl. None of the other colors would help them accomplish the goal. Explain that in life we have to make choices, and not all choices will help us get to the temple.

Challenge

With your parents or church leaders, discuss some of the requirements of obtaining a temple recommend.

Challenge

This week, I will learn about some of the requirements of obtaining a temple recommend.

_____

Signature

_____

Date

Family history work connects me to my ancestors.

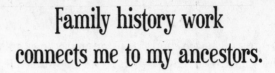

Resources

(Select one from each category.)

Children's Songbook
+ Family History—I Am Doing It (94)
+ Families Can Be Together Forever (188)

Hymn
+ High on the Mountain Top (5)
+ We Love Thy House, O God (247)

Gospel Art Book
+ The Nauvoo Temple (118)
+ Temple Baptismal Font (121)

Scriptures
+ Matthew 16:19
+ 1 Peter 3:19

Lesson

The family is central to the plan of salvation. Heavenly Father wants us to be connected not only to our immediate family but to also our extended family and ancestors. How do we connect ourselves to those whom we have never met and have already passed on?

Family history work provides us with that opportunity. We can do the temple work for our ancestors and be sealed to them. We can also ask our parents and other family members what they remember about our ancestors. Some people are lucky enough to have journals and histories written by their ancestors. They can read about their ancestors' lives and learn about how they gained a testimony or overcame trials.

How is your family doing your family history?

Read and discuss Malachi 4:6.

+ Who are the children and who are the fathers in this verse?
+ How will their hearts be turned to each other?

Activity

All Ages: With the help of your parents, fill out a four-generation pedigree chart. You can download one at http://store.lds.org/images/estore/products/eng/334_01616000_o06.pdf.

Challenge

Get in the habit of writing in your journal so that one day your children and grandchildren can learn about your experiences. This week, write in your journal at least three times.

Challenge

I will write in my journal at least three times this week.

_____
Signature

_____
Date

July

We Become Members of the Church through Baptism and Confirmation

The Church of Jesus Christ has been restored.

Lesson

Resources

(Select one from each category.)

Children's Songbook
+ The Church of Jesus Christ (77)
+ On a Golden Springtime (88)

Hymn
+ High on the Mountain Top (5)
+ Hark, All Ye Nations! (264)

Gospel Art Book
+ Missionaries: Elders (109)
+ Missionaries: Sisters (110)

Scriptures
+ Revelation 14:6
+ 3 Nephi 16:7

When Jesus Christ was on the earth, He gave the priesthood keys to His Apostles. That means that after Jesus returned to Heavenly Father, the Apostles had the authority, or power, to act in Jesus's name and continue to lead His Church. But there were many wicked people on the earth who did not want to follow Jesus and belong to His Church. They killed the Apostles, and after the Apostles were gone, no one had the authority to lead the Church of Jesus Christ.

For hundreds of years, the Church of Jesus Christ was not on the earth. People still believed in Jesus Christ and formed other churches, but no one had the authority to act for Jesus Christ. None of these churches was the true Church of Jesus Christ.

Thankfully, in 1830, the Church of Jesus Christ was restored through the Prophet Joseph Smith. Joseph Smith received all the priesthood keys to lead the Church, and today we have the fulness of the gospel. God has promised that He will never again take the priesthood from the earth.

Read and discuss Doctrine and Covenants 132:45.

+ What has God restored?
+ What does God mean when He says He will "make known unto you all things in due time"?

Activity

All Ages: Watch *The Restoration*, available at http://www.lds.org/media-library/video/feature-films.

Challenge

This week mention the Church to a friend in one of your conversations. You can invite someone to church, but this challenge can be as simple as mentioning that you attend church each Sunday.

Challenge

This week, I will mention the Church in one of my conversations with my friends.

_____
Signature

_____
Date

Week TWO

I become a member of the Church through baptism and confirmation.

Lesson

Resources

(Select one from each category.)

Children's Songbook
* When Jesus Christ Was Baptized (102)
* The Holy Ghost (105)

Hymn
* Lead Me into Life Eternal (45)
* Lord, Accept into Thy Kingdom (236)

Gospel Art Book
* Girl Being Baptized (104)
* The Gift of the Holy Ghost (105)

Scriptures
* Acts 2:38
* 3 Nephi 12:2

Last week we talked about the Church of Jesus Christ. Heavenly Father wants all of us to become members of the true church. To do so, we must be baptized by a priesthood holder and confirmed a member of the Church.

As soon as you turn eight, you can be baptized. Baptism is a very important step that we must take to return to Heavenly Father. When we are baptized, we make sacred covenants with Heavenly Father. We promise Him we will keep His commandments, and He promises to forgive us for our sins.

After we are baptized, a Melchizedek Priesthood holder lays his hands upon our heads and confirms us members of The Church of Jesus Christ of Latter-day Saints. He also gives us the gift of the Holy Ghost. If we keep the commandments and repent when we sin, the Holy Ghost will be our constant companion. He will comfort us, guide us, reveal truth to us, and help us feel the love of Heavenly Father and Jesus Christ.

Read and discuss our baptismal covenants in Mosiah 18:8–10.

- ✦ What do we promise Heavenly Father when we are baptized?
- ✦ What does Heavenly Father promise to do for us?

Activity

Younger Children: See page 74.
Older Children: See page 75.

Challenge

If you have been baptized, write about your experience in your journal. What do you remember about that special day? Who baptized you? Who came to witness it? How did you feel? If you have not been baptized, write about (or draw a picture of) what you are looking forward to most about your baptism and what you can do to prepare for it.

Challenge

This week, I will write about my baptism in my journal.

_____

Signature

_____

Date

Great to Be Eight

Children can be baptized when they are eight years old. Can you find the two number 8s below that look exactly alike?

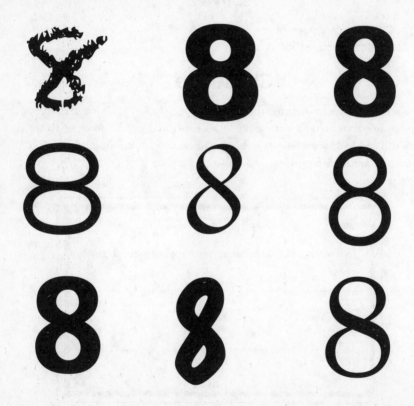

Word Scramble

Unscramble the words below. When you are finished, discuss with your parents how they relate to this week's lesson. *Solution on page 142.*

1. VOENNCTA

2. GIHTE

3. MMRSIOINE

4. HYOL HGOTS

5. RHCURC

6. SUSEJ

The Holy Ghost comforts and guides me.

Lesson

Nephi and his brothers faced many challenges when they tried to obtain the brass plates from Laban. First, Laban stole the valuable items the brothers offered Laban for the plates. Then Laban tried to kill them. Laman and Lemuel were angry, but Nephi knew they could not give up. Nephi went to Laban's house again, having faith that he would be guided and protected. He said, "And I was led by the Spirit, not knowing beforehand the things which I should do" (1 Nephi 4:6). Nephi was in a scary situation, but he knew the Holy Ghost would comfort him and guide him.

If we are worthy, the Holy Ghost will comfort and guide us. When we need help, He will guide us in making the right decision. When we are sad, He will help us feel the love of Heavenly Father and Jesus Christ.

People feel the Holy Ghost in different ways. Some people hear a still, small voice. Others have thoughts come into their minds or feel strongly that they should do something. No matter how we feel the Holy Ghost, we will always feel good when the Holy Ghost is near.

Read (or summarize) and discuss 1 Nephi 4:7–38.

+ How did the Holy Ghost help Nephi?
+ How has the Holy Ghost guided and protected you?

Activity

All Ages: Play sounds your children are familiar with that signify an event: the phone ringing, the doorbell, the car starting, a timer, someone knocking at the door, an alarm clock ringing, and so forth. Explain that these signs all represent something that is taking place. For example, when the phone rings, we know someone wants to talk to us. When an alarm clock rings, it is time to get up. Liken this to the promptings of the Holy Ghost. When we feel peace, the Holy Ghost is telling us to go ahead and do something. When we have a stupor of thought or a bad feeling, the Holy Ghost is warning us not to do something.

Challenge

This week, practice listening to the still, small voice. After you say your personal prayers at night, sit quietly for a few minutes and listen to the promptings of the Holy Ghost.

Challenge

I commit to sit quietly after I say my personal prayers and listen to the promptings of the Holy Ghost.

_____

Signature

_____

Date

I can know the truth through the power of the Holy Ghost.

Lesson

It can be difficult to know if what we are taught is true. But God does not want us to remain confused. He has promised to send the Holy Ghost to help us.

When Lehi took his family into the wilderness, Nephi and his brothers wondered if their father really did have a vision that Jerusalem would be destroyed. Even though Nephi was righteous, leaving his home was difficult. But he prayed to know if his father's words were true, and the Holy Ghost comforted him and told him that they were (see 1 Nephi 2:16–17).

We can do the same. Whenever we have doubts about something being true (the scriptures, the words of the prophets, and so forth), we can pray and ask God. He will send the Holy Ghost to tell us what is right.

Read and discuss Moroni 10:3–5.

+ When we want to know the truth, do we simply ask God, or do we need to do something else first?
+ How does the Holy Ghost manifest truth?

Resources

(Select one from each category.)

Children's Songbook
+ Search, Ponder, and Pray (109)
+ The Holy Ghost (105)

Hymn
+ Testimony (137)
+ I Know My Father Lives (302)

Scriptures
+ John 15:26
+ 3 Nephi 11:36

Activity

Younger Children: Before family home evening begins, write a message to your children with invisible ink: Dip a Q-tip or paintbrush in some milk and write a message on a piece of paper. During family home evening, give your children the message written in invisible ink. Turn the stove on low, and help them hold it about twelve inches above the burner until the message appears. (If the message does not appear, you may need to turn up the heat; however, be careful not to light the paper on fire.) Explain to your children that the heat from the stove is like the Holy Ghost. He helps us to see things that are not obvious and tells us the truth of all things.

Older Children: See page 80.

Challenge

Before you go to Primary next Sunday, say a special prayer and ask Heavenly Father to help you know that the things you will be learning are true. Pay attention to how you feel during Primary. Do you feel peace? Do you have a warm feeling inside? This is the Holy Ghost telling you the gospel is true.

Challenge

Before I go to Primary next Sunday, I will say a special prayer and ask Heavenly Father to help me know that the things I will be learning are true.

_____
Signature

_____
Date

Crossword Puzzle
THE HOLY GHOST

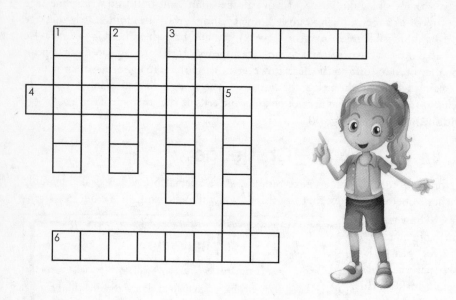

ACROSS
3. Third member of the _____
4. _____ us of sin
6. _____ us when we are sad

DOWN
1. Manifests the _____ of all things
2. Speaks in a still, small _____
3. Protects and _____ us
5. Is a personage of _____

August

Participating in Wholesome
Activities Will Strengthen
My Family

"Pray in your families unto the Father"

Lesson

Jesus Christ taught the Nephites, "Pray in your families unto the Father, always in my name, that your wives and your children may be blessed" (3 Nephi 18:21). What do you think He meant? What types of blessings can we pray for?

The Church leaders have counseled us to pray as a family each morning and each night. When we do this, our love for each other grows and our bonds are strengthened. When we pray together for the same things, we become more unified and can feel the Spirit together.

We have also been counseled to pray individually, and husbands and wives should pray as a couple. This gives us an opportunity to pray for other family members and to seek personal guidance.

Jesus also taught us to "pray always, lest ye be tempted by the devil, and ye be led away captive by him" (3 Nephi 18:15). Prayer brings us a spiritual power that we can't get anywhere else.

Resources

(Select one from each category.)

Children's Songbook
- A Child's Prayer (12)
- I Pray in Faith (14)

Hymn
- Did You Think to Pray? (140)
- Sweet Hour of Prayer (142)

Gospel Art Book
- Young Boy Praying (111)
- Family Prayer (112)

Scriptures
- 1 John 3:22
- Alma 37:37

Read and discuss Alma 34:19–27.

+ Where and when should we pray?
+ What are some of the things we can pray for?

Activity

Younger Children: Read Matthew 7:7–12. Then act out the scenario presented in this passage.

Older Children: See page 84.

Challenge

Praying together is one of the most important things we can do as a family. Set a goal with your family to have family prayer both morning and night every day this week.

Challenge

Each day this week, my family and I will have family prayer both morning and night.

_____
Signature

_____
Date

Word Search

Below is the passage of scripture that we read during our lesson. Find the words in bold in the word search on the following page. *Solution on page 142.*

19 Yea, humble yourselves, and continue in **prayer** unto him.

20 Cry unto him when ye are in your fields, yea, over all your **flocks**.

21 Cry unto him in your houses, yea, over all your **household**, both morning, mid-day, and evening.

22 Yea, cry unto him against the power of your **enemies**.

23 Yea, cry unto him against the **devil**, who is an enemy to all righteousness.

24 Cry unto him over the **crops** of your fields, that ye may prosper in them.

25 Cry over the flocks of your **fields**, that they may increase.

26 But this is not all; ye must pour out your souls in your **closets**, and your secret places, and in your wilderness.

27 Yea, and when you do not cry unto the Lord, let your **hearts** be full, drawn out in prayer unto him continually for your welfare, and also for the **welfare** of those who are around you.

```
O T A C S A A C V Q K Q Z V A G S
J A P W V N S C V J O E J W A C S
M W L U E D F L O C K S C M I F U
L X V S I C U E L P T B I Z U M Y
O V G B W K V N Z N R F F V V A E
O R W I M I H E G P W C Q M K J W
D S H K C W C M W E L F A R E W M
E Z O O G R A I U H O P P J C D Y
D V U O J G H E A R T S R R P U R
E C S F S O K S H L H N T A K J H
V C E S N E V W P J F W U S Y F J
I L H B Y R Z L I A X U P E Q E T
L O O O V B V L V L A O O Z M Z R
T S L X E W E F P E R P N C Q N R
F E D V V K U E C C F W K C E F X
S T V X B G F V F I E L D S S Q E
J S L V U N A U I W Q F X S O F V
```

Family home evening strengthens my family.

Lesson

Resources

(Select one from each category.)

Children's Songbook
- The Family (194)
- Family Night (195)

Hymn
- Home Can Be a Heaven on Earth (298)
- Families Can Be Together Forever (300)

Gospel Art Book
- Family Prayer (112)

Scriptures
- Deuteronomy 6:7
- Moses 5:12

Do you look forward to having family home evening each week? What do you like about it? It's fun spending time together as a family, but there's more to it than fun activities and treats. The prophets have counseled us to have family home evening to strengthen our families. When we spend time together learning about the gospel, our testimonies grow together and we become more united. Family home evening is also a time when we can set goals as a family and work together to achieve those goals. In addition, setting aside one day each week just for our family shows our family members that we love each other and are committed to each other.

Read and discuss John 13:34.

- How can we show love to our family members?
- How does having family home evening strengthen our love for each other?

Activity

All Ages: Play Bed Sheet Ping Pong. Divide your family into two teams. Each team holds one side of a bed sheet. Place a ping pong ball in the middle of the sheet. Each team shakes the sheet and tries to get the ball to fall off the sheet from the other team's side. Each time the ball falls off the sheet, the team who shook it off gets a point. The first team to earn five points wins. After the game is over, discuss the importance of teamwork and working together as a family.

Challenge

Set a goal with your family to hold family home evening every week for a month. At the end of the month, discuss how family home evening has helped your family.

Challenge

My family and I will hold family home evening each week for a month.

_____
Signature

_____
Date

Scripture study gives me and my family spiritual strength.

Lesson

How do you feel after eating a good breakfast? Do you feel strong and ready to tackle the day? Heavenly Father has given us food to fuel our physical bodies, and He has given us another type of food to fuel our spirits: the scriptures.

Studying the scriptures each day gives us the spiritual strength that we need to choose the right. But the word *study* is a very important word. If we just read the scriptures quickly, without giving them much thought, we won't receive the strength that we need. It's like eating only a couple bites of cereal and then running out the door and expecting to do well at school.

In the Book of Mormon, the prophet Nephi said that we should "feast upon the words of Christ" (2 Nephi 32:3). Let's read about that in 2 Nephi.

Read and discuss 2 Nephi 32:3.

+ What does it mean to "feast upon the words of Christ"?
+ What will the words of Christ tell us?

Resources

(Select one from each category.)

Children's Songbook
+ Search, Ponder, and Pray (109)
+ The Books in the Old Testament (114)

Hymn
+ As I Search the Holy Scriptures (277)
+ Thy Holy Word (279)

Gospel Art Book
+ Joseph Smith Seeks Wisdom (89)

Scriptures
+ Isaiah 34:16
+ D&C 11:22

Activity

Younger Children: Draw a picture of your favorite scripture story.
Older Children: Have a scripture chase using scriptures that relate to the family. Look in the Topical Guide for ideas.

Challenge

Have family scripture study every day this week. Determine a time that you will study the scriptures, and make that your top priority during that time. At the end of the week, discuss with your family how studying the scriptures together has strengthened your family.

Challenge

My family and I will have family scripture study each day this week.

_____
Signature

_____
Date

The Sabbath is a day of rest and worship.

Lesson

Heavenly Father has set apart the Sabbath day (Sunday) as a day of rest and a time when we can focus on worshiping. The most important thing we can do on the Sabbath day is attend all our church meetings and partake of the sacrament. But after we come home from church, we should still focus our thoughts on Heavenly Father.

Many of the activities we do during the week are not appropriate to do on Sunday. For example, if possible, parents should not go to work. We shouldn't shop or go to movies or sporting events.

Instead, we should do things that help us grow in the gospel or grow together as a family. We can read the scriptures or Church magazines, visit the sick, write in our journals, call family members who live far away, or do family history.

We may feel like we have to give up a lot on Sunday, but Heavenly Father will bless us if we keep the Sabbath day holy. Let's read about some of those blessings in the scriptures.

Read and discuss D&C 59:9–19.

+ How can we keep the Sabbath day holy?
+ What blessings will we receive for honoring the Sabbath day?

Activity

All Ages: Sometimes it can be hard to find things to do on Sunday afternoon. As a family, put together a Sabbath Day Kit. Find a box or a backpack and fill it with activities that are appropriate for the Sabbath day: a journal and a pen, stationery to write letters, appropriate books, appropriate music, and so on. You can make one kit for the entire family or one kit for each child.

Challenge

Next Sunday, practice keeping the Sabbath day holy. Resist the temptation to go to the store, play sports, and do other activities that you shouldn't do on Sunday. Use the Sabbath day kits that you made during family home evening.

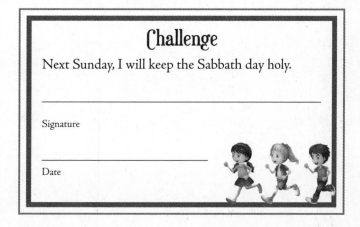

Challenge

Next Sunday, I will keep the Sabbath day holy.

_____
Signature

_____
Date

September

Living the Gospel
Blesses My Family

I show my gratitude by showing thanks for all my blessings.

Lesson

Resources

(Select one from each category.)

Children's Songbook
+ Thank Thee for Everything (10)
+ Thank Thee, Father (24)

Hymn
+ All Creatures of Our God and King (62)
+ I Stand All Amazed (193)

Scriptures
+ D&C 78:19
+ Alma 34:38

How do you feel when you give someone a present or do something nice for them and they don't say thank you? That's how Heavenly Father feels when we don't thank Him for our blessings. In the Doctrine and Covenants, we learn that ingratitude (not showing thanks) is one of the greatest sins (see D&C 59:21).

But there is more to gratitude than just saying, "Thank you." Imagine that your parents bought you a brand new bike for your birthday. You were excited when you received it and told them thank you, but then you never rode it and acted like you didn't have a bike. Your parents would feel sad and disappointed that you didn't like their gift.

Heavenly Father is sad when we don't read the scriptures or attend church. He has blessed us with many ways to draw closer to Him, and we need to show Him how grateful we are to have Him in our life.

Read and discuss D&C 29:21.

+ Why do you think ingratitude is such a great sin?
+ How can we show our gratitude to Heavenly Father?

Activity

Younger Children: Write a thank you note to someone who has blessed your life. (If you don't know how to write yet, you can draw a picture or have your parents help you write it.)

Older Children: Make a gratitude poster. Write a list or draw pictures of things that you are grateful for. Hang it somewhere your family will see it often, and continue to add to it throughout the week.

Challenge

Each time you pray this week, thank Heavenly Father for three things. (Be sure to thank Him for your blessings before you ask for help.)

Challenge

This week, I will thank Heavenly Father for three things each time I pray.

_____
Signature

_____
Date

Resources

(Select one from each category.)

Children's Songbook
+ When We're Helping (198b)
+ "Give," Said the Little Stream (236)
+ I Have Two Little Hands (272)

Hymn
+ Because I Have Been Given Much (219)
+ You Can Make the Pathway Bright (228)

Gospel Art Book
+ Service (115)

Scriptures
+ Mosiah 2:17
+ D&C 42:29

By giving service to others, I give service to God.

Lesson

When Jesus was on the earth, He taught that those who will be saved at the last day are those who serve others.

Read and discuss Matthew 25:34–40.

+ What did Jesus mean when He said, "Inasmuch as ye have done it unto one of the least of these my brethren, ye have done it unto me"?
+ How can we serve our family members?
+ How are we serving God when we serve each other?

Activity

All Ages: Do a service project as a family. You could pick up trash at a park or school, help a neighbor with yard work, or even take a meal to someone in need.

Challenge

Do a secret act of service for someone this week.

Challenge

This week, I will do a secret act of service for some-one.

_____

Signature

_____

Date

We believe in being honest.

Lesson

Resources

(Select one from each category.)

Children's Songbook
+ The Thirteenth Article of Faith (132)
+ I Believe in Being Honest (149)

Hymn
+ Oh Say, What Is Truth? (272)
+ Truth Reflects upon Our Senses (273)

Scriptures
+ 2 Nephi 9:34
+ D&C 51:9

The first sentence of the thirteenth article of faith states, "We believe in being honest." What does it mean to be honest? Most people think of honesty as telling the truth. Not lying is a big part of honesty, but there's more to it than that. We need to be truthful in our actions as well as in our words.

You probably know that it is wrong to cheat in school or to steal. Did you know that cheating and stealing are forms of dishonesty? Other forms of dishonesty include pretending to be someone we are not or leading someone to believe something that is only half true.

At times, it can be very difficult to be honest. Sometimes being honest will get us in trouble. But no matter how much trouble we may get in, we should always tell the truth. Heavenly Father will be proud of us for being honest, and He will bless us for our efforts.

Read and discuss Articles of Faith 1:13.
+ What does it mean to be honest?
+ How do you feel when people are not honest with you?

Activity

Younger Children: Color the picture on page 100.
Older Children: See page 101.

Challenge

Sometimes it is easy to exaggerate when we're telling our friends about one of our experiences. When we exaggerate, we feel that our story is more exciting. However, we need to remember to be honest. This week, make a special effort not to exaggerate and to relate stories exactly as they happened.

Challenge

This week, I will make a special effort not to exaggerate. I will strive to be honest in all that I do and say.

_____
Signature

_____
Date

Being **honest** means playing **fairly** and **not cheating.**

Missing Vowels

THIRTEENTH ARTICLE OF FAITH

Below is part of the thirteenth article of faith. Fill in all the missing vowels to discover what it says about honesty. *Solution on page 142.*

W__ B__L__ __V__ __N B__ __NG

H__ N__ ST, TR__ __ , CH__ ST__ ,

B__ N__ V__ L__ NT, V__ RT__ __ __ S,

__ ND __ N D__ __ NG G__ __ D T__

__ LL M__ N.

A A A

E E E E E E E E E E E

I I I I I I   O O O O O O O

U U U

Resources

(Select one from each category.)

Children's Songbook
+ Jesus Wants Me for a Sunbeam (60)
+ Dare to Do Right (158)

Hymn
+ Each Life That Touches Ours for Good (293)
+ Teach Me to Walk in the Light (304)

Scriptures
+ John 13:15
+ 3 Nephi 15:12

By living the gospel I set a good example for others to follow.

Lesson

When Jesus gave the Sermon on the Mount, He said, "Let your light so shine before men, that they may see your good works, and glorify your Father which is in heaven" (Matthew 5:16). The light that Jesus was referring to is your testimony and example. He doesn't want you to hide your testimony of Him. He wants you to show the world what Christlike love is through your actions. When you live the gospel and help others (do "good works," as Jesus said), you set a good example for others to follow. Without using words, you teach others how to be kind, honest, and obedient.

People often don't comment on how we act, but they do notice how we behave. It is important that we always try our best to represent Jesus Christ. We never know how we may touch someone's life with our good example.

Read and discuss 1 Timothy 4:12.
+ Can you be a good example even if you are very young?
+ In what ways can you be a good example?

Activity

Younger Children: See page 104.
Older Children: See page 105.

Challenge

Find an opportunity this week to be a good example. If your siblings are fighting, don't participate. If the other kids in Primary are chatting and not paying attention, sit reverently and set a good example.

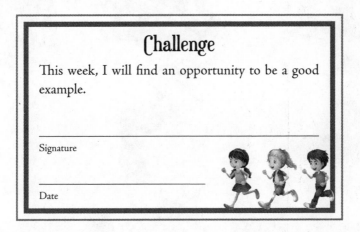

Challenge

This week, I will find an opportunity to be a good example.

_____
Signature

_____
Date

I Can Be a Good Example

Which children are being a good example? Circle the ones who are being good examples, and put an X on the ones that aren't.

Hangman

Use some of the phrases below (or create your own) to play Hangman with your family. Each completed puzzle will tell your family what you can do to be a good example. If possible, use a chalkboard or dry erase board so everyone can see. A large piece of paper will also work.

GO TO CHURCH

PRAY OFTEN

DO MISSIONARY WORK

OBEY PARENTS

READ THE SCRIPTURES

PAY TITHING

HELP THE POOR

VOLUNTEER OUR TIME

BE BAPTIZED BY IMMERSION

BE KIND TO OTHERS

GO TO THE TEMPLE

ATTEND PRIMARY ACTIVITIES

RESPECT GOD'S CREATIONS

HOLD FAMILY HOME EVENING

OBEY THE WORD OF WISDOM

LISTEN TO GOOD MUSIC

WATCH GOOD MOVIES

OBEY CHURCH LEADERS

RESPECT OTHERS

October

"The Family: A Proclamation to the World" Came from God to Help My Family

"The Family: A Proclamation to the World" came from God.

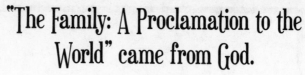

Lesson

Resources

(Select one from each category.)

Children's Songbook
+ Love Is Spoken Here (190)
+ Because God Loves Me (234)

Hymn
+ O My Father (292)
+ Love at Home (294)

Gospel Art Book
+ Young Couple Going to the Temple (120)

Scriptures
+ "The Family: A Proclamation to the World"

Many people in the world do not believe that families are important anymore. However, the prophets teach us differently. In 1995, the First Presidency and Council of the Twelve Apostles wrote a proclamation (letter) to the world. In it, they talked about how important families are to God's plan.

President Hinckley read the proclamation during the General Relief Society meeting in Salt Lake City. He stated that "marriage between a man and a woman is ordained of God and that the family is central to the Creator's plan for the eternal destiny of His children." The proclamation also mentions that each family member has sacred responsibilities.

Let's read the proclamation and discuss what we learn from it.

Read and discuss "The Family: A Proclamation to the World."

+ Why are families central to God's plan?
+ Why do you think the prophet and apostles gave this proclamation to the world?

Activity

All Ages: Watch the video of President Hinckley presenting the "Proclamation" to the Relief Society. It is available at https://www.lds.org/general-conference/1995/10/stand-strong-against-the-wiles-of-the-world?lang=eng.

Challenge

Give a copy of "The Family: A Proclamation to the World" to a friend or neighbor (you can print it from www.lds.org).

Challenge

This week, I will give a copy of "The Family: A proclamation to the World" to a friend or neighbor.

_____
Signature

_____
Date

Marriage between a man and a woman is essential to God's plan.

Resources

(Select one from each category.)

Children's Songbook
+ I Love to See the Temple (95)
+ Where Love Is (138)

Hymn
+ Families Can Be Together Forever (300)
+ Love One Another (308)

Gospel Art Book
+ The Salt Lake Temple (119)
+ Young Couple Going to the Temple (120)

Scriptures
+ "The Family: A Proclamation to the World"
+ Genesis 2:24

Lesson

The first paragraph of "The Family: A Proclamation to the World" states, "We, the First Presidency and the Council of the Twelve Apostles of The Church of Jesus Christ of Latter-day Saints, solemnly proclaim that marriage between a man and a woman is ordained of God and that the family is central to the Creator's plan for the eternal destiny of His children."

Marriage between a man and a woman is essential to God's plan. When Adam and Eve were in the Garden of Eden, God married them as husband and wife. Adam and Eve were the first example of a loving husband and wife who obeyed the Lord's commandments.

The prophets have taught that marriages can be eternal (last forever) if they are performed by the proper authority. When a man and a woman are sealed in the temple, they will remain married to each other even after they die. Their children will also be theirs for eternity. The doctrine of eternal marriage is one of the most beautiful parts of the gospel. After the Atonement of Jesus Christ, our families are our most precious gift from Heavenly Father.

Read and discuss 1 Corinthians 11:11.

+ Why is marriage between a man and a woman essential to God's plan?
+ How can a marriage be eternal?

Activity

All Ages, Option 1: Look at wedding photos of your parents or grandparents. Talk about the importance of marriage.

All Ages, Option 2: Look at pictures of different temples on www.lds.org. Discuss why a temple marriage is essential to Heavenly Father's plan.

Challenge

Talk to your parents or another married couple. Ask them about the blessings they have received from being married.

Challenge

This week, I will talk to my parents or another couple about the blessings they have received from being married.

_____
Signature

_____
Date

When family life is founded on Jesus's teachings, we can be happy.

Lesson

Resources

(Select one from each category.)

Children's Songbook
+ Because God Loves Me (234)
+ Here We Are Together (261)

Hymn
+ How Firm a Foundation (85)
+ From Homes of Saints Glad Songs Arise (297)

Gospel Art Book
+ Jesus Knocking at the Door (65)
+ The Second Coming (66)

Scriptures
+ Helaman 5:12
+ D&C 6:34

When Nephi and his family were searching for the promised land, the Lord told them, "Inasmuch as ye shall keep my commandments ye shall prosper in the land; but inasmuch as ye will not keep my commandments ye shall be cut off from my presence" (2 Nephi 1:20). The same promise applies to each of us. When we obey the commandments, Heavenly Father will bless us.

Following the teachings of Jesus Christ brings great joy. It is impossible to choose the right and feel bad. Sometimes choosing the right is hard—and we may have to give up something we want very much—but Heavenly Father will bless us for choosing the right. We may not see the blessings immediately, but they will always come.

Read and discuss Doctrine and Covenants 82:10.

+ Why is the Lord bound when we do what He says?
+ What does it mean to "have no promise"?
+ What are some of the blessings our family has received for following the teachings of Jesus Christ?

Activity

All Ages: Give each child two pieces of paper. Have them draw a happy face on one and a sad face on the other. Then read the statements on page 116 to your children. Have them decide if the family is following the teachings of Jesus Christ. If so, your children should hold up the happy face. If not, they should hold up the sad face.

Challenge

As a family, pick one of Jesus Christ's teachings that you would like to practice. During the week, do something as a family that will help you practice it. For example, if you want to be more charitable, you could read scriptures about charity and then help someone in need.

Challenge

This week, I will help my family practice the following teaching of Jesus Christ:

_____

_____

Signature

_____

Date

Resources

(Select one from each category.)

Children's Songbook
+ A Happy Helper (197)
+ When We're Helping (198)

Hymn
+ Have I Done Any Good? (223)
+ The Time Is Far Spent (266)

Scriptures
+ Genesis 3:19
+ John 5:17

Successful families work together.

Lesson

Heavenly Father has taught us that working is important. He wants us to be responsible and provide for ourselves and our families. In the Doctrine and Covenants, the Lord said, "Thou shalt not be idle; for he that is idle shall not eat the bread nor wear the garments of the laborer" (D&C 42:42). This scripture means that if we do not work, we should not expect to receive the rewards others have from working.

Successful families work together. It takes a lot to run a household. Parents are responsible for providing food, shelter, and clothing for their families. Children should help with chores that are appropriate for their age. Work doesn't have to be boring. If we have a good attitude and understand its purpose, we can enjoy it. And, most important, working together as a family builds strong relationships.

Read and discuss 2 Nephi 5:17.
+ What does it mean to be industrious?
+ How can we work together as a family?

114

Activity

All Ages: Do a chore or project together. Make it fun by telling stories or singing songs while you work. Afterward, have a treat or play a game as a reward.

Challenge

Have you heard the saying, "Many hands make light work"? When we work together, our chores get done quickly, and no one is burdened with all the work. This week, offer to help a family member with a chore so that you have more time to spend with each other.

Challenge

This week, I will offer to help a family member with a chore.

_____
Signature

_____
Date

When family life is founded on the teachings of Jesus Christ, we can be happy.

See page 113 for directions.

1. This family attends church every Sunday.

2. This family usually goes to church, but sometimes they miss it to attend sporting events.

3. This family likes to go out to eat after church on Sunday.

4. This family gets up early to read the scriptures together before work and school.

5. This family prays together daily.

6. This family has decided that they don't have enough money to pay tithing.

7. This family helps their elderly neighbor with his yard work once a week.

8. This family fasts if they aren't hungry when they wake up on fast Sunday.

November

Living the Teachings of
Jesus Christ Strengthens
Me and My Family

"If ye have faith, ye have hope"

Resources

(Select one from each category.)

Children's Songbook
+ I Pray in Faith (14)
+ Faith (96)

Hymn
+ Testimony (137)
+ I Know My Father Lives (302)

Scriptures
+ 2 Corinthians 5:7
+ D&C 63:10

Lesson

In the Book of Mormon, the prophet Alma taught, "If ye have faith ye hope for things which are not seen, which are true" (Alma 32:21). We cannot see Heavenly Father and Jesus Christ, but we can have faith that they are real. We cannot see the prophets from the scriptures, but we can have faith that they were good men and taught the word of God. We do not know what will happen in the future, but we can have faith that God will bless us with what we need.

Faith in Jesus Christ is the first principle of the gospel. Without faith, we cannot repent or become members of the Church. Without faith, we cannot find purpose in going to church or obeying the commandments. Sometimes it is difficult to believe in things we can't see, but each time we use our faith, it will grow.

Read and discuss Alma 32:28.
+ How is faith like a seed?
+ How can we make our faith grow?

Activity

Younger Children: Plant a seed in a small pot or a paper cup. Water it according to the package instructions and check on its progress daily. Discuss with your family how taking care of this seed is like nourishing your faith.
Older Children: See page 120.

Challenge

This week, do something that is difficult for you. Ask Heavenly Father to help you and then exercise your faith in Jesus Christ to do it.

Challenge

This week, I will do something difficult and will ask Heavenly Father for help.

_____
Signature

_____
Date

Secret Code

Using the key below, decode the message on the next page. *Solution on page 142.*

A =
B =
C =
D =
E =
F =
G =
H =
I =
J =
K =

L =
M =
N =
O =
P =
Q =
R =
S =
T =
U =
V =

W =
X =
Y =
Z =

Prayer is reverent communication with Heavenly Father.

Lesson

Resources

(Select one from each category.)

Children's Songbook
+ I Pray in Faith (14)
+ Faith (96)

Hymn
+ Testimony (137)
+ I Know My Father Lives (302)

Scriptures
+ 2 Corinthians 5:7
+ D&C 63:10

Has your father ever gone on a trip without you? How did you feel? Did he seem far away because you couldn't see him? If you were able to talk to him on the phone, you were probably very excited to tell him about what was happening in your life. Do you ever feel that Heavenly Father is far away because you can't see Him? It may seem that way at times, but Heavenly Father is only as far away as we make Him. We can always talk to Heavenly Father through prayer, and the Holy Ghost will tell us that He's listening.

Heavenly Father wants us to pray to Him each day. He wants to know what is going on in our lives, and He wants us to ask Him for help. We can pray to Heavenly Father to know if the scriptures are true, or we can ask Him to help us find something that we lost. We should also pray and give thanks to Heavenly Father. Everything that we have comes from Him, and we need to show that we are grateful. Even though we may not hear Heavenly Father's voice speaking to us when we pray, we can feel the Holy Ghost. This is Heavenly Father's way of letting us know that He hears our prayers.

Read and discuss Doctrine and Covenants 19:28.

+ What does it mean to pray in your heart?
+ How does Heavenly Father hear us, even when we don't pray out loud?

Activity

Younger Children: Make a telephone with soup cans and string (see page 124 for instructions). Go in different rooms and take turns talking to each other. Explain to your children that even though we can't see Heavenly Father, we can pray to Him anytime, anywhere. He will always hear and answer our prayers.

Older Children: See page 125.

Challenge

It's easy to get into the habit of saying the same thing each time we pray. The scriptures teach us that we should not do this. This week, make a special effort to make each prayer unique (different).

Challenge

This week, I will make a special effort to make each prayer unique (different).

_____
Signature

_____
Date

Can You Hear Me?

Materials

2 identical soup cans
pointed tool*
5-foot length of string
toothpick (optional)

Instructions

1. In the bottom of each can, punch a small hole. The hole should be big enough for the string to go through but small enough that it won't fall out when knotted.
2. Insert the string through the hole in one of the cans. Tie a knot and pull string tight. If the knot is not big enough and the string slips through the hole, tie the string around a piece of toothpick to hold the string in place.
3. Repeat step 2 with the remaining can and the other end of the string.

* To avoid injury, parents should help children punch holes with the pointed tool.

We must listen carefully so we can hear the answers to our prayers.

Prayer from A to Z

Each family member needs his own copy of this paper. Set the timer for two minutes. Write down all the things you can pray for from A to Z. Whoever comes up with the most wins.

A_____   N_____

B_____   O_____

C_____   P_____

D_____   Q_____

E_____   R_____

F_____   S_____

G_____   T_____

H_____   U_____

I_____   V_____

J_____   W_____

K_____   X_____

L_____   Y_____

M_____   Z_____

Repentance is a change of mind and heart.

Lesson

Resources

(Select one from each category.)

Children's Songbook
+ Help Me, Dear Father (99)
+ Repentance (98)
+ The Fourth Article of Faith (124)

Hymn
+ Come unto Jesus (117)
+ As Now We Take the Sacrament (169)

Scriptures
+ 2 Nephi 2:21
+ D&C 58:42

The only way to return to Heavenly Father is to follow Jesus Christ and keep all the commandments. But when He sent us to earth, Heavenly Father knew we would not always choose the right. He provided a Savior for us so we can repent of our sins and be forgiven. Because Jesus Christ died for us, we can be washed clean from our sins.

We must take certain steps to be forgiven. First, we admit that we made a mistake and feel godly sorrow for our sins. That means we feel sad that we sinned and wish we hadn't done it. There is a difference between feeling godly sorrow and feeling sorrow because we have to face the consequences of our sins.

Second, we forsake, or stop, our sins. If we have lied, we must stop lying. If we have been unkind to someone, we must stop being unkind.

Third, we confess our sins to Heavenly Father and anyone else that we want to forgive us. If we called someone a bad name, we must confess that sin to both Heavenly Father and the person we hurt.

Fourth, we make restitution. That means we try to correct the wrong act. If we have stolen something, we return the item to the owner or find a way to pay for it.

Fifth, we forgive others. God cannot forgive us if we don't forgive others.

Finally, we keep the commandments of God. We are not fully repentant if we don't continue doing our best to choose the right. We must have a change of heart and lose our desire to sin.

Repentance can be hard, but we will find great joy in giving up our sins and following Jesus Christ.

Read and discuss Isaiah 1:18.
+ What are scarlet and crimson?
+ How does the turning of these colors to white represent repentance?

Activity

All Children: Put a lemon in a bowl of water and explain to your children that lemons float in water. Push the lemon down to show that it will pop back up and float. Cut the lemon in small pieces. The pieces will still float. Then remove the skin from each piece of lemon. The pieces will now sink. Liken the lemon to ourselves and repentance. The skin of the lemon is like our sins. As long as we are holding on to our sins, we cannot truly repent and be cleansed. But when we shed our sins, we can "sink" into the water, just like the pieces of lemon did, and be cleansed from our sins.

Challenge

(*See page 130.*)

Week
FOUR

Resources

(Select one from each category.)

Children's Songbook
+ Repentance (98)
+ The Fourth Article of Faith (124)

Hymn
+ Prayer Is the Soul's Sincere Desire (145)
+ Father in Heaven, We Do Believe (180)

Gospel Art Book
+ The Crucifixion (57)
+ The Lost Lamb (64)

Scriptures
+ Psalm 38:18
+ Alma 34:33

Forgiveness brings peace.

Lesson

In the Book of Mormon, we read about a man named Enos and his experience with repentance. One day, Enos was hunting in the forest and started thinking about the gospel truths that his father, Jacob, had taught him. Enos felt a great desire in his heart to repent of his sins. He knelt down in the forest and began to pray. Let's read about his experience.

Read and discuss Enos 1:4–8.
+ How did Enos know his sins were forgiven?
+ Why was his guilt swept away?

Activity

All Ages: Have a child wear an empty backpack. The other children take turns putting a rock, a book, or another heavy object inside. As each item is placed in the backpack, the child names a sin (name-calling, disobeying parents, and so on). When the backpack is full, ask the child to walk across the room. He may not be able to do it, and if he can, it will be difficult.

128

Explain how sins weigh us down and make it hard for us to "walk" back to Heavenly Father. Then, one by one, remove each "sin" from the backpack. Explain how repentance lightens our load and brings peace. You may want to read Matthew 11:28 and discuss how the Savior carries our burdens.

Challenge

Are you holding a grudge? How does it make you feel when you don't forgive someone? This week try to readily forgive everyone who offends you. You'll be a much happier person if you do! It can be hard sometimes to forgive others. Don't forget that you can always pray and ask Heavenly Father for help.

Challenge

This week, I will readily forgive anyone who offends me.

_____

Signature

_____

Date

Challenge

(Continued from page 127)

Choose one bad habit to repent of this week. Remember, repenting is more than just saying you're sorry. It includes feeling sorrow for your sin, confessing it to God, asking for forgiveness, making restitution (fixing the wrong), and forsaking the sin (never doing it again). If we sincerely do all these things, we will receive forgiveness for our sins.

Challenge

This week, I commit to make my prayers to Heavenly Father more sincere. I will express my gratitude, tell Him about my day, and ask for help when I need it.

_____
Signature

_____
Date

December

We Remember and Worship Our
Savior, Jesus Christ

The sacrament is a time to remember Jesus Christ.

Lesson

Resources

(Select one from each category.)

Children's Songbook
+ To Think about Jesus (71)
+ Before I Take the Sacrament (73a)

Hymn
+ As Now We Take the Sacrament (169)
+ While of These Emblems We Partake (173)

Gospel Art Book
+ Blessing the Sacrament (107)
+ Passing the Sacrament (108)

Scriptures
+ John 6:54
+ D&C 59:9

When we are baptized, we promise to follow Jesus Christ. As much as we want to follow Him, we still sin afterward. Fortunately, we can always repent of our sins. We should repent often, even daily if necessary.

Each Sunday, we renew our baptismal covenants when we take the sacrament. Although we are baptized only once, we can recommit (promise again) each week to choose the right.

You have probably noticed that the chapel is very quiet during the sacrament. That is because the sacrament is a sacred ordinance. We need to focus our thoughts on Jesus and think about how we can better follow Him. And we need to be quiet so that those around us can do the same.

During the sacrament, some people read from the hymn book or from their scriptures. Others like to just think about what Jesus Christ means to them. Whatever you choose to do, make sure that your thoughts are focused on Jesus and His sacrifice for us. Think about what you can do that week to be a better disciple of Jesus Christ.

Read and discuss the sacrament prayers in Doctrine and Covenants 20:77, 79.

+ What covenants do we renew when we take the sacrament?
+ What does God promise us if we keep our covenants?

Activity

All Ages: Make Christmas cards to send to friends or relatives. Include your testimony of the Savior.

Challenge

Next Sunday, listen carefully during the sacrament prayers. Sit reverently while the sacrament is being passed and think about the words of the prayers.

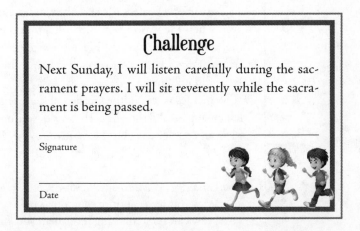

Challenge

Next Sunday, I will listen carefully during the sacrament prayers. I will sit reverently while the sacrament is being passed.

_____

Signature

_____

Date

Week TWO

Remembering Jesus Christ helps me choose the right.

Lesson

Resources

(Select one from each category.)

Children's Songbook
+ Stand for the Right (159)
+ Choose the Right Way (160)

Hymn
+ Do What Is Right (237)
+ Choose the Right (239)

Gospel Art Book
+ Christ's Image (1)
+ Christ with Children (116)

Scriptures
+ Joshua 24:15
+ Psalm 119:30

Each day, we are faced with choices. We must decide if we will pray that day, read the scriptures, be obedient, be kind to others, and so on. Sometimes we may be tempted to do other things instead. When we remember Jesus Christ's example, it will be much easier to choose the right.

Jesus lived a perfect life and always chose the right, even when He was in very difficult situations. When He fasted for forty days, He was extremely hungry. Satan tempted Him to turn stones into bread. But Jesus did not give in.

When Jesus was in the Garden of Gethsemane, He felt great pain. All the sins of the world were upon Him. He wanted to give up, but He wanted to obey Heavenly Father more. Let's read about His experience.

Read and discuss Matthew 26:36–39.
+ Why did Jesus endure such great pain?
+ How can remembering Jesus help you choose the right?

Activity

All Ages: Bake Christmas cookies or another treat to deliver to your neighbors.

Challenge

Memorize the Primary song, "Jesus Once Was a Little Child." Sing it to yourself when you are tempted to make a wrong choice.

Challenge

I will memorize the Primary song, "Jesus Once Was a Little Child."

_____
Signature

_____
Date

Week THREE

Resources

(Select one from each category.)

Children's Songbook
* Once within a Lowly Stable (41)
* Away in a Manger (42)

Hymn
* Joy to the World (201)
* O Little Town of Bethlehem (208)

Gospel Art Book
* The Road to Bethlehem (29)
* The Birth of Jesus (30)

Scriptures
* Isaiah 59:20
* 3 Nephi 11:10

The Son of God was born on earth.

Lesson

Read and discuss the story of Christ's birth in Luke 2:1–19.

* Why did the angel tell the shepherds not to fear?
* Why was Jesus born in a manger?

Activity

Younger Children: Look at the picture on page 138. Retell as many details as you can about the story of Christ's birth.

Older Children: Look at the picture on page 138. In the space provided on page 139, write as many details as you can about the story of Christ's birth.

Challenge

Write your testimony in the front cover of a Book of Mormon. Give it to one of your friends or to the full-time missionaries to give to an investigator.

Challenge

I will write my testimony in the front cover of a Book of Mormon and give it to:

_____

_____

Signature

_____

Date

Jesus Christ's Birth

_____

_____

_____

_____

_____

_____

_____

_____

_____

_____

Jesus Christ will come again.

Resources

(Select one from each category.)

Children's Songbook
*   When He Comes Again (82)
*   The Tenth Article of Faith (128)

Hymn
*   The Spirit of God (2)
*   Now Let Us Rejoice (3)

Gospel Art Book
*   The Second Coming (66)

Scriptures
*   2 Thessalonians 1:7
*   D&C 1:12

Lesson

After Jesus was resurrected, He taught His disciples that even though He would soon return to His Father, He would come to earth again. But no one would know when that would be. Jesus, said, "But of that day and hour knoweth no man, no, not the angels of heaven, but my Father only" (Matthew 24:36).

Latter-day prophets have taught that the Second Coming will take place soon. But we still do not know when that day will come. We need to live righteously and be ready to meet Jesus. It will be a glorious day for those who are prepared.

When Jesus comes again, He will establish His kingdom here on earth. We must be prepared for that day because only the righteous will remain on the earth. Even though we don't know exactly when Jesus will return, we have many scriptures that tell us which signs to look for.

Read and discuss Matthew 24. (It's a long chapter, so read it beforehand and select verses to read with your family.)

- What are some of the signs of the Second Coming?
- How can we prepare for it?

Activity

All Ages: Celebrate the end of the year and the beginning of a new year by playing your family's favorite game and making your favorite treat.

Challenge

This week, watch the news or read the newspaper with your parents and discuss some of the events that show the Second Coming is drawing near. However, remember the Savior's counsel in Matthew 24:6: "Be not troubled: for all these things must come to pass, but the end is not yet."

Challenge

This week, I will watch the news or read the newspaper with my parents and discuss some of the events that show the Second Coming is drawing near.

_____
Signature

_____
Date

Answer Key

PAGE 5

1. I
2. AM
3. A
4. CHILD
5. OF
6. GOD

PAGE 39

1. UNITY
2. LOVE
3. BROTHER
4. MOTHER
5. SISTER
6. HOME
7. FATHER
8. FAMILY

PAGE 85

PAGE 11

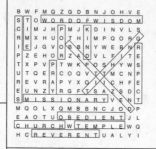

PAGE 75

1. COVENANT
2. EIGHT
3. IMMERSION
4. HOLY GHOST
5. CHURCH
6. JESUS

PAGE 101

WE BELIEVE IN BEING HONEST, TRUE CHASTE, BENEVOLENT, VIRTUOUS, AND IN DOING GOOD TO ALL MEN.

PAGE 34

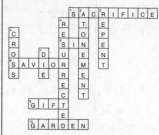

PAGE 80

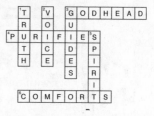

PAGE 121

IF YE HAVE FAITH YE HOPE FOR THINGS WHICH ARE NOT SEEN, WHICH ARE TRUE

Fun Food for FHE

Simple, Kid-Friendly
Recipes

*These recipes may not be fancy, but they're
simple, fun foods that children of all ages will
enjoy making and eating.*

Popcorn Cake

¾ cup butter
2 (16-oz.) bags marshmallows
12 cups popped popcorn (remove unpopped kernels)
2 cups peanut butter M&Ms
1 cup pretzels, broken into small pieces

1. Melt butter and marshmallows in a large saucepan.

2. Mix in popcorn. Let cool a few minutes.

3. When cool, stir in M&Ms and pretzels. Mix with your hands, if necessary.

4. Press mixture firmly into a buttered cake pan.

Frozen Hot Chocolate

4 oz. chocolate, finely chopped
2 tsp. hot chocolate mix
1½ cups milk
3 cups ice

1. Melt chocolate in a saucepan.

2. Stir in hot chocolate mix.

3. Remove from heat. Add ½ cup milk and stir until smooth. Let mixture cool to room temperature.

4. Place chocolate mixture, 1 cup milk, and ice in a blender. Blend on high speed until smooth.

5. Pour into glasses. Top with whipped cream and chocolate shavings, if desired.

Caramel Apple Dip

1 can sweetened condensed milk

1. Pour sweetened condensed milk into a pot.
2. Cook on medium-low heat, stirring continuously (10–15 minutes).
3. Remove from heat when it thickens to your desired consistency.

S'mores Bars

½ cup peanut butter
graham crackers
2 bananas, chopped
½ cup chocolate chips
½ cup white chocolate chips
1 cup mini marshmallows

1. Spread peanut butter on graham crackers.

2. Line a 9x13 baking sheet with graham crackers.

3. Sprinkle bananas and chocolate chips over graham crackers. Top with mini marshmallows.

4. Cover with foil and bake at 350 degrees for 15 minutes. Remove foil and bake an additional 5 minutes, or until marshmallows are nice and toasty.

Cake Batter Cookies

      1 box cake mix
      ½ cup vegetable oil
      ½ cup water

1. Mix together all ingredients.
2. Spoon onto ungreased cookie sheet and bake at 350 degrees for 10–12 minutes.

Variation: Add 1½ cup chocolate chips, raisins, or nuts.

Waffle Cones

4 waffle cones
2 cups yogurt
2 cups chopped fruit, assorted varieties

1. Fill each cone with a spoonful of yogurt.

2. Add a spoonful of fruit to each cone. Repeat layers until each cone is full.

Ice Cream Sandwiches

1 box cake mix
eggs, oil, and water (amount varies with each mix)
your favorite ice cream

1. Prepare cake mix according to package directions.

2. Bake individual portions of the mix in a waffle iron instead of in the oven.

3. Allow the waffles to cool to room temperature. Cut each waffle in half and spread with ice cream. Place the other half on top to create a sandwich.

Dessert Kabobs

12 strawberries, washed and hulled
12 banana chunks
12 marshmallows
12 brownie chunks
6 wooden skewers

Thread each skewer with fruit, marshmallows, and brownie chunks. Alternate shapes, colors, or textures.

Mini Apple Pie

1 cup apples, chopped
1 tsp. cinnamon
1 tsp. sugar
6 Tbsp. cream cheese
3 graham crackers, broken in half

1. Mix together apples, cinnamon, and sugar. Cook on high in the microwave for 1 minute.
2. Spread 1 tablespoon cream cheese onto each graham cracker half. Top with a spoonful of apple mixture.